"The Girls" Guide to Money Etiquette

For Money Etiquette Questions please visit
www.professormoneymanners.com

"The Girls"
Biography

"That was the worst flight I've ever been on. You two should seriously consider a different profession!" was the comment the disgruntled passenger made to us as he exited the plane. He wasn't completely out of line expressing his disdain towards us, after all we'd spent the entire transcontinental flight sequestered in the galley power chatting about life, love and the passenger in 3A who was drooling on his necktie. It was the first time we had flown together, but instantly knew we had a bond that would surpass most ordinary friendships. The time flew by so quickly, we were shocked when the captain announced, "prepare for landing." Not long after that initial flight, we came to the conclusion that it was time to turn in our wings. Luckily that didn't impact the alliance we'd built, rather it became the foundation for our connection that included other similar interests and phases of life including marriage, child rearing and co-authoring a book.

The idea for **"The Girls" Guide to Money Etiquette,** was the result of being frustrated by money being the biggest downer of the evening. Whether it was a collective dining experience that left us mesmerized at how the check panned out or how to comfortably talk about money without looking materialistic, there were countless times we would find ourselves analyzing the situation. We were smart enough to know we couldn't be the only ones appalled at other people's money manners, or lack thereof, and started to keep a mental journal of all the encounters we endured when money reared its ugly head. "Oh, this is one for the book," we would say. Well, lo and behold we wrote that book! We took a stance and provided edgy etiquette advice for all sorts of money debacles.

Our personal bios have taken drastic turns from each other, but the core of our chemistry remains intact. We joke that with each passing year we are morphing into one person. Our husbands feel like they've joined the ranks of polygamy getting two wives for the price of one. The children have become confused as to who is their "real" mother, given the lines have blurred at which child is sleeping at whose house, and due to the fact that on any given day either one of us might show up for carpool duty. Over time we have unintentionally taken on each others personas, from having the same hair style to dressing alike and even thinking alike...hence the reason our other friends have given us the moniker "The Girls."

Introduction

You may be asking yourself, "What do two girls who used to push peanuts for a living know about money?" A great question. It's funny, after over 25 years of being flight attendants, a friendship that has spanned a decade and a brood of children between us, we've gained enough experience to realize that money and relationships are a fragile mix. "FASTEN YOUR SEATBELT," this may be a bumpy ride..."

$$\text{\$}$$

Gals, are your friendships leaving you bankrupt? We love our "girl-time," but what happens when money becomes the awkward entity to a fabulous girl's night out? Nothing sours a meal faster than struggling over finances at the end of a terrific evening.

Money is never cut and dried. Whether dining out, traveling together, or just plain chit-chatting, money can leave us feeling more exhausted than the Daylight Savings Time change. **We love our friendships,** but money tends to annoy, frustrate, and rattle even the tightest of bonds. Maybe it's hanging out with someone who is "slow on the draw but quick on the thank-you," or perhaps the constant "price dropping" of our pal is causing us angst, and everyone knows a perpetual moocher (who frankly needs to be handled with special care). Regardless of the situation, we don't want money to be the root of a lost friendship.

Let's face it: Emily Post needs a make-over to incorporate money manners. Knowing the secrets to **"everything money"** helps take the focus off the accounting and gives us more time to spend on truly important girl stuff . . . like admiring our new aviator sunglasses. This is the first guide book that gives us what we need, answers that apply to our sexy, sassy lives. **(Shhhh keep this to ourselves, don't tell the boys.)**

Table of Contents

"Check Please!"

Collective Dining

In Flight Entertainment: The Last Supper

When we were flight attendants, it often

perplexed us how serious passengers got over the meal. In the off chance we ran out of chicken or beef, (okay, there was more than an off chance), people would go ballistic. (This is the mystifying part. You're in coach. It's chicken. Or beef. Not coq au vin. Or prime rib). "I want the chicken!" "Sir, I understand you want the poultry hockey puck, but I ran out of that delicious selection a few rows back." You've seen these types on the plane, the ones who actually insisted that we find a parachute, jump out of the plane, and then somehow catapult ourselves back after we grab him a chicken McWhatever from the nearest Golden Arches. Funny thing, he asked for seconds.

"It's Only One Meal"

Food. There is so much pressure on keeping trim, looking fabulous, and staying healthy; but **A GIRL'S GOTTA EAT**, right? If counting calories isn't tedious enough for us, reconciling the bill can be an even bigger equation. It wasn't always this way, back in junior high the highlight of the weekend was walking down to the Dairy Queen and indulging in greasy fries followed by a chocolate dipped cone. Ah, the beauty of guilt-free eating. As a kid, these trips to fast food joints with our cheer squads didn't produce any money dilemmas. We pooled our allowances then stuffed ourselves with junk food. We ate until we barely squeezed into our uniforms. Around the time we no longer needed that uniform, it became apparent that money, especially when bill sharing, could be an *awkward* issue.

Rule 1: Don't let a perfectly good evening be clouded by an uncomfortable struggle over paying the check; you have enough to worry about just figuring out how to afford the Jimmy Choo shoes you can't live without. The focus of dining out shouldn't be about the money, but should be about everyone ogling your new pumps.

"How Should We Pay?"

The New York Split: the amount is divided equally by the number of people.

The Itemized Deduction: getting out your calculator and divvying up exactly what each person ordered, cross referencing with wallet-sized tip chart.

Taking the Hit: one person pays the entire bill. Simple, clean and lovely.

There are benefits and pitfalls to each style. Depending on who you're dining with, how often you dine together and the personal level of your relationship will dictate which option is the least intrusive.

Rule 2: Let's not nit-pick, it'll all even out. We often hear the complaint among Non-Drinkers who feel shafted when they're put in the position of having to pay for part of someone else's cocktail. To compensate they will order the fried calamari, bowl of clam chowder and the extra large slab of cheesecake to compensate for not ordering booze. Apparently sparing the liver (which periodically regenerates itself) is more important than having to undergo a quadruple bypass.

Julianne's Incident: a small price 2 pay

The New York Split (my personal favorite) is probably not the most equitable financially, but limits the amount of squabbling over who had what. This quick split requires little attention and puts the focus back on what's enjoyable; socializing over a meal. Once I was having a much-needed pow-wow with my girls, gorging on comfort food and drowning my sorrows over a recent unexpected weight gain. Of course, scarfing carbohydrates isn't helping, a vicious cycle indeed, but it felt good in the moment. (Tried the Atkins Diet once. Lost ten pounds in two weeks. Then ate one grain of rice and promptly blew up like a balloon again). Anyhow, when the bill came, Merideth (the consummate perfectionist) insisted on not doing a New York Split since she drank only iced tea while Heidi and I drank a few beers. I looked at Heidi with that "Oh-my-God-are-you-kidding-me expression? Is she really going to insist we divide the four-sixty-three difference?" Oh yes she was. Doing a New York Split would have cost Merideth an additional buck-sixty: a small price to pay for making bill sharing seamless.

Rule 3: Use the Itemized Deduction method sparingly. There's nothing worse than enjoying a splendid evening with a fascinating group of people, having the bill arrive, then someone starts the sorting out of the who owes what. Here we go... First of all, people have a tendency to underestimate what they owe, shocking considering their house and car is always quoted as double, but when it comes to their entrée it seems to be a depreciating asset.

Heidi's Incident: A little lite!

There's a dark side to the New York Split, on the occasion when the division isn't equitable at all (okay, so this isn't a perfect science). As a single flight attendant and living on a modest income, I rarely treated myself to an elaborate meal. One specific time, I was invited to dinner with a group of gals. Even though I was light on funds, typical end of the month problem for me, I really wanted to get out. The mishap between my blow-dryer and round brush left me a bit frizzy, but I managed to make it to the restaurant missing the first few rounds of drinks and appetizers. I sat down and asked the waitress for a small dinner salad and water. Have you done this? Ordered a meal so tiny the garnish was larger than the portion? Anyway...

I spent a few hours chatting while the table enjoyed a full dinner, drinks and dessert. When the check arrived, one of the girls did a quick tally and opted for the New York Split. It was $100 per person! I'm sure most of the girls expected this amount after their smorgasbord, but for me it seemed a bit excessive for a $12 salad. I ever so s-l-o-w-l-y counted out my twenties hoping someone would notice that I only ate a leaf of lettuce and an mini cherry tomato, and insist on taking me out of the equation. No such luck. The cash was snatched up so fast it made the skin fly off my fingertips!

The point: If you're committing to commonly dine, prepare to perhaps pay for more than you ordered. And remember, when you dine with an assorted group, you may not have control over the chosen method of payment.

Rule 4: Cash is King! We are smart, independent and financially savvy ladies. Bringing cash makes the bill sharing smoother than your flat ironed hair. Especially when you're part of a large party, please, please bring cash. Nothing is worse than having several credit cards thrown into the pile prolonging an otherwise quick split of the check. Luckily there are ATM machines on practically every corner that are just chomping at the bit to take your two dollar and seventy-five cent service fee. Always come to a group dinner with cash.

If avoiding a bill fiasco is your priority, then Taking the Hit is a worthwhile option. There are a few things to keep in mind if Taking the Hit appeals to you. First, make sure that when it's your turn to pay, you're buying a comparable dinner. In other words, if you're treated to a **seafood extravaganza complete with Chardonnay and a view of the Pacific,** don't think the next time you're at the "Feed-n-Fuel" paying the tab there satisfies your obligation.

Another pitfall to Taking the Hit lands on the person who's being treated. Most employed, rational people don't want to feel like a **freeloader.** We've experienced countless times when someone offering to pay is confronted by his or her dining companions resisting the generosity. Heidi once saw a lady's plastic Lee Press On nail go flying across the table in her attempt to snap up the bill first. The literal pulling back and forth over whose turn it is to pay can send even the waiter packing, or make it necessary for him to don riot gear.

Just Say "THANKS!"

> **Rule 5:** Always offer to pay your portion, just once. There's an appropriate amount of exchange that needs to take place once someone offers to Take the Hit. If your offer is declined, there are three ways in which you can say "Thank you;" Reciprocal, Noncommittal and Humor.

Noncommittal: You can simply say "thanks," and mention something positive about the meal. "Thanks for dinner, that was the best chicken Marsala I've ever had." This option doesn't open the door in the event that you don't want to pay the next time. Or even have a next time, like the blind date your friend swore looked like George Clooney; Oh yeah, he looked like George

Clooney, if George shaved his head into a dome pattern, grew a monobrow and gained fifty pounds.

Reciprocal: This allows you to thank your host and assures them that you're game with taking the hit next time. In the event that your date really DOES look like Clooney and you want to secure a second outing, "Thanks for picking that up; next time it's on me. How's Thursday?" So smooth.

Humor: If all else fails you can always resort to your quick wit. "Thanks for picking up the check. You're free again next Tuesday, right?"

Rule 6: Taking the Hit means picking up the entire bill (tip included, yes included) for everyone at the table. Don't get us wrong, someone offering to pay the tip is generous, but it has the potential to complicate the split. The beauty of Taking the Hit is to make it simple.

"So, what if I'm really hungry?"

Our friend Colleen loves to dine and feels free to order a cocktail before dinner, a variety of appetizers, and always ends her meal with dessert and coffee. Colleen isn't rude or expecting someone else to pay her way, she just gets tired of eating Lean Cuisines by herself all week. She's conscientious of her choice to order-up, and acts accordingly when the bill comes. **Regardless of the method of payment**, Colleen will always throw in more. Even if we insist on a New York Spilt, she will matter-of-factly announce that she doesn't want to feel guilty for her indulgences and will toss in extra cash. Sometimes we leave her extra to a really great server, other times we take the money right off the top and split the balance. The beauty is Colleen doesn't feel pressured to act like a "Roman." Therefore, we're not offended when she orders in excess.

Similarly to Colleen, Julianne's husband isn't a fan of behaving like a Roman. Being an amateur wine connoisseur (We'd love to say "mostly sewer," but he's actually pretty good), he often indulges in ordering rare wines. When he chooses his vintage selection, he will quietly ask a waitress to put the bottle on a separate tab. This way he can enjoy sharing his **Chateau-Le-Snob** without imposing a hefty price on his dining companions. Funny, this is the same guy who ordered White Zin on their first date.

Rule 7: Resist the urge to over order. When in Rome, do as the Romans do. In other words, eat like a pig when dining with swine's. If everyone's ordering drinks and a three course meal, then indulge and enjoy. Likewise, if you're going for a quick bite with friends, this is not the time to order a reserve wine. But if you can't help yourself, then BUCK UP and pay!

The end of a meal is always marked by a moment of turmoil. First off, there is the struggle as to whether or not you should indulge in an ever-so-tiny bite of chocolate molten lava cake knowing you've already exhausted all of your "points" for the day, next there is the matter of deciding if there is a reminisce of your dinner prominently displayed between your two front teeth, but mostly it is the split second when the waiter sets down the check. Do you wait to see who reaches first? Do you pretend like you didn't notice the obvious arrival? Or do you confront it, head on, and risk the possible aftermath of side effects?

Oh, the possibilities!

Slow on the Draw but Quick on the Thank You: the type who will let the bill sit, and sit, and sit, send a text message, reapply her already overly glossed lips; anything to not have to pick up that tab. But as soon as it's paid, wow, she's the FIRST to say "thanks".

The Dine and Dasher: always have precise timing and clever excuses as to why they need to run. They conveniently leave before the bill arrives because they need to "get home to their babysitter". They've advanced way beyond how we used to think of Dine and Dashers, you know, the kids who would ditch the check then run out of the restaurant, gambling no one would chase them down. They always say they'll get it the next time, but interestingly next time never comes.

Showy People: always insist on paying, the "I'm-so rich-and-successful-don't-you-wish-you-were-me" Showy.

Rule 8: Don't leave the wrong impression. Keep in mind, the cost could be higher than the meal itself. Repeat after us: "You can't put a price on great friendships!"

Ladies, in the interest of keeping all costs at bay, **come to dinner prepared for anything.** If the money doesn't pan out exactly, or if the method of split isn't your preference, don't give it a second thought. Finally, if you're watching your weight by ordering lightly, and others decide to go for the "all you can eat lobster feast," the extra money spent out of pocket is better than the extra pounds you might have to burn off later. Think of how great you'll look in your True Religion jeans.

Rule 9: Most of all, let it go! Don't let improper money etiquette take away from the luxury of dining out. Remember, it's just one meal, one evening and one bill.

Tips at a Glance

❖ Choose a split that makes paying seamless

❖ Don't let money become the reflection of the evening

❖ Regardless of financial equitability, let it go

"Jet Lag"
Traveling

In Flight Entertainment: Marry Me, Fly Stand-by

One of the best perks to being a flight attendant is flying for free, actually it's stand-by and many times it turns out to be more money than the cost of a confirmed seat. It's especially tricky when more than one stand-by is traveling together, in the event there is only one seat left on the plane. This happened to us a few years back when we had this grand idea to fly to Miami (during spring break). We got bumped off the first direct flight to Miami. No problem, we'll just take the next flight (an all-nighter), connect in Dallas and land in Florida only a few hours past our original plan. We arrived in Dallas, ran quickly thru half the terminal to our connecting gate and then saw the crowd. "Doesn't look good," was the agent's response to us. "You'd better try the next flight to Fort Lauderdale." We ran twenty-three gates to the next flight, and good news, they had space. The bad news was just one seat. "You go, I'll catch the next one." Heidi said. Sounds cruel not to stick together, but that's the thing about stand-by, you get there anyway you can (the wing, overhead bin and lavatory are all viable options at this point.) I landed in Ft. Lauderdale, took a bus to Miami, checked into the hotel and went directly to the computer to see if Heidi had made the next flight. Nope, not that one, or the next six flights! And she was trying for any city within a 300 mile radius. In the end, after twenty-four hours of getting bumped off of flights, we bought her a full-fare ticket. A costly endeavor, both in price and time...**not exactly "free!"**

The best part of traveling is sharing the experience with friends. As wonderful as sipping drinks by the pool, enjoying an art museum or shopping at a local street fair turned out to be, traveling with others is also a potential landmine for money becoming an issue.

"You don't really know a person until you've taken a vacation with them."

It scared our friend Christy to death the first time she took a trip with her future husband, when he carefully displayed his toiletries in alphabetical order on the vanity. Two things crossed her mind: being chopped up into little pieces and stuffed in a hefty bag, and preparing to act nonchalant if he turned the light switch on and off three times before exiting a room. Thankfully neither occurred, he was just a bit of a metrosexual. Of course, personal conflicts can always occur with any new romance or social situation. But because most people don't travel alone, this chapter is designed to help avoid having money be the **biggest misconnect of your trip**.

Rule 10: Know your travel companion's budget. Vacations are a luxury. There are vast differences in people's financial situations, so when traveling with others, an individual's finances need to be considered.

Julianne's Incident: Tight Budget

When my husband and I were first married, we were asked to join another couple for a week long getaway to the Big Island of Hawaii. Although a vacation was not in our immediate plans, the picture perfect scenery they described sounded magical. Receiving stand-by airline seats as a job perk made the escape seem affordable. Oh, how naïve I was.

When I called to book the hotel, I nearly fainted when I was told by the reservations agent that the least expensive room was a staggering $800 per night (and no, that didn't include breakfast!) It was so far out of our price range it was comical. Putting my pride aside, I called my close friend and joked that the only way we could go was if the hotel charged by the hour. At nearly a grand a night, we could only afford about a half-hour vacation stay.

Budget is Everything!

Rule 11: Know what you can afford. It's easier to say "no" before you leave than spend your vacation stressing over money.

Heidi's Incident: Movin' on UP!

Being on the same financial page was essential when we planned a Savers vacation with another family to The Bahamas. Having small children, we agreed that we were on a tight budget and sharing a condominium near the beach would be ideal. We would also share a minivan, limit our dinners out and cook in the condo. We made the plan. Our budget was in check. We all agreed . . . we were Savers. We were vacationing in The Bahamas with our good friends and kids. What more could we want? Well, I was about to find out...remember my mentioning we were near the beach? That's real estate lingo for, "pack your cooler, load your gear (including stroller, beach chairs and sand toys), get into your rental car and drive one mile to the public beach". After the first day of schlepping to the water, we decided to try the condo pool. It was located in the complex. How far could that be? After walking about a mile with our overloaded strollers and cranky toddlers, we finally arrived at the "aquatics center." Picture a small square pool, plastic chairs and a soda machine behind a chain link fence. Our view was not of the Bahamian sunset, but of the exclusive resort next door. While we sat on the hot cement (all six chairs were already occupied), we peeked into the Grand Hotel where we saw children cruising down hundred-foot water slides, cabanas filled with fresh fruit and waitresses with frothy frozen drinks topped with festive little umbrellas. All of the sudden, our vacation didn't seem appealing at all. Although both families had agreed on the frugal budget, it was at that precise moment we decided we were actually Loungers. We wanted to be at the resort enjoying all the perks. If we wanted to cook and lug our kids around, we could have stayed home. Realizing each other's limited funds, we pooled our resources, ditched the condo and squeezed both families into one standard room at the lush resort. To this day, we joke about how we must have looked like the "Beverly Hillbillies," sharing a room at this exclusive hotel. We were Loungers on a Savers budget, or "$20 Millionaires" as we would laughingly refer to ourselves later.

Rule 12: It is recommended that everyone you're traveling with is of the same money mindset.

"How Do You Decide the Budget?"

Deciding the budget can make or break that much needed vacation. The way we see it there are three types of vacationers: **Doers, Loungers, and Savers.** There is no "right" way to travel, but if you're with someone who wants to budget different from you, it can make the vacation go all "wrong!"

The players:

Doers prefer to spend their vacation budgets on fun activities such as safaris or deep sea fishing. These people see vacations as an opportunity to have a new experience (often at the physical level). Most Doers are not concerned with their accommodations stating, "We're never in the room anyway." They're more interested in exploring exciting destinations.

Loungers lean toward resort destinations featuring fancy spas, fine dining and **delicious towel boys** who spritz you with water. Loungers are looking to escape the hustle and bustle of everyday life. They are over-packers who insist that every outfit needs to have a matching pair of shoes. Never having to leave the resort on their stay is a slice of heaven.

Savers are those individuals who really want to vacation, but simply aren't willing to spend their hard earned money on amenities that can cause the price of a trip to skyrocket. These people choose budget motels, eat where the locals hang out and rent cheap mopeds to see the sites. Their attitude is, "You don't need to spend a fortune to gain the experience of a fabulous destination." They are delighted when a cruise costs them a fraction of what it costs the other passengers because they chose to forgo a window cabin for an indoor bunk on the engine floor. **"I had the same meals, went to the same ports and enjoyed the same shows as the other fools who paid a mint to have a miniature hole they call a window!"** The value of the vacation does not require spending a lot of cash. It's free to see Stonehenge, the Smithsonian or Niagara Falls.

"Vacation's are a Luxury!"

A lot goes into planning a vacation. When traveling with friends, it can become complicated organizing travel arrangements. Usually a person emerges from the group who becomes the **"Cruise Director."** This is the person who is wonderful at researching all the best places to go, finds the cheapest fares and ends up booking the entire package. Befriend this personal concierge. All other travelers simply need to worry about packing their bags and writing a check for what they owe.

"We Love Julie McCoy!"

Rule 13: Be aware of the cruise director's out-of-pocket expenses. Many times they will get stuck with surcharges or extra fees when booking the arrangements.

If being out a couple of bucks puts a damper on the vacation planner, nothing stings as much as the **"no show."** How many times have you been sitting around a backyard barbecue and someone says, **"We should all rent a beach house this summer."** In the moment, everyone is on board. The next day, after the margaritas have worn off, it becomes evident who was serious and who was just letting Jose Cuervo do the talking. It's fine to reconsider at that point, but once you commit (sober), others financially depend on your participation. If you get a rash from a painful bikini wax and cancel, you still need to pay. This may sound outlandish, but we were at that particular barbecue, and found Julianne emerging as the Cruise Director. The day after the barbecue Julianne began to make the plan. Three families committed to the summer house. She put the entire nonrefundable week on her credit card and trusted everyone would reimburse her. The day before we were beach bound, one of the wives apparently got a bum pedicure and ended up with a foot fungus (seriously). She left a message on Julianne's voicemail backing out of the trip, never mentioning her third of the rental. After a few attempts to recoup the cost of her flaking out, we were left to cover the difference.

RULE 14: Collecting money up front discourages people from canceling and alleviates the financial burden of the Cruise Director.

"What's the best way to share trip expenses?"

The Kitty:

A common pot where each person contributes a designated amount of money. Food, drinks, snacks and even toilet paper are paid for from this fund. It works especially well when house sharing. If the kitty runs dry, each family throws in another Ben Franklin. At the end of the trip, the remaining cash is split evenly (meow!).

The Purse (the Super Kitty)

Entire trip expenses being paid by the common pot. One person is responsible for the substantial bank-roll for the girls. Every time we need to grab a cab, pay an admission to a club, tip a doorman or pay any bill, the purse holder says, "Don't worry gals, I got it." It's better than having a sugar daddy on the trip! The "purse" allows us to pay up front then never feel awkward about "whose-going-to-cover-what" during the entire trip.

Traveling is hectic enough. "What time is my flight, did I pack my prescription and will my luggage make the connection?" are all valid concerns when vacationing. Alleviating worry over money is one way to take the focus *off* of finances and *on* what really counts . . .

enjoying the escape!

Tips at a Glance

❖ Decide on your budget

❖ Travel with those who have the same vacation vision

❖ If you commit, pay your portion (regardless)

❖ A common pot simplifies sharing

"Chit Chat"

Talking About Money

In Flight Entertainment:
Not so Friendly Skies

There are two types of flight attendants, "A" scale and "B" scale. Basically, once you've hit the "A" scale, you are now making above the poverty line. Ordinarily it is rude to talk about how much someone earns for a living, but the blatant conversations regarding what scale someone is obscures any etiquette normally practiced. Ironically the new hires, making the least amount of money, are often times the most energetic of the bunch (we adore flying with new hires that, "love to travel and enjoy working with people.") It's refreshing that they are untarnished and so willing to help passengers with a big smile and warm welcome. That is why it was unfortunate when poor Shelly, our star new-hire let a passenger get the best of her. During taxi on an "all-nighter" from NYC to LAX, Shelly diligently passed out all the pillows and blankets, like a good stew should. Regrettably, she ran out just before the aft section of coach. A very tired and cranky man **insisted** she find him another. Not possible, they were all out. The man began to verbally accost Shelly, to the point that she burst into tears, looked him directly in the eye and said, "Do you realize I only make like $14,000 a year? I can tell you this abuse isn't worth it...I QUIT!" And she did. And he got nothing the rest of the flight.

At an early age, we learn that it's impolite to talk about money. That is basically the long and short of our education regarding chatting about money. This chapter is a departure from some parents' mantra: **don't discuss money, politics or religion.** Guiding us to be non-partisan agnostics is good advice for avoiding debates at cocktail parties, if that's your primary goal, but does little to teach us how to handle the awkwardness of money. Because, we are more or less ill prepared, people often suffer the blunders of talking too much, too little or too awkwardly about money.

Types of Talkers:

The Price Dropper: someone who voluntarily provides price tags along with conversation.

The Asker: someone who directly asks the cost of something.

The Bushman: A person who uses the round-a-bout tactic of making inferences that essentially say the same thing as the price. "Beats around the Bush."

The Highballer: A person who exaggerates the cost of something for purposes of leaving an impression.

The Lowballer: Someone who down plays the cost of things in order to avoid looking ostentatious.

> **When interacting with price droppers,** unless you keep yourself abreast of general economics, you could really portray yourself as looking ignorant. **We like to give the ambiguous nod with raised eyebrow reaction that could mean,** "Wow, I'm surprised you got such a good deal, or "Wow, I can't believe you had to pay so much." Either way, we're covered.

Annoying chatter about money can also come in the opposite form of the Price Dropper. The "Askers," have guts. They find nothing wrong with directly asking the cost of something. (There is a tiny part of us that finds this refreshing, after all what's the big secret of hiding the information, given almost everything can be looked up on the internet anyway.)

Rule 15: Try to avoid being an "Asker." Inquiring how much something costs is, in most cases, viewed as poor money etiquette.

There are also those individuals who *want* you to ask them, just dying for you to ask them how much they paid. "Guess how much this cost? Come on guess, guess!" Again, this puts people in a pickle. Why not just ask them to guess your age too? And while they're at it, why not guess our weight! There is not a response that wins. You look stupid either way, guessing too high or too low. Duh!

THE BUSHMAN will elude, hint and even use the term "X amount," holding the number hostage at all costs. They literally BEAT around the money bush. Etiquette speaking, they're right. There really never is a reason to give a number, but socially speaking it becomes distracting trying to follow the code. I wonder if the BUSHMAN realizes that once you decipher the cryptogram, it's pretty clear on how much they spent.

When people discuss prices there are usually those who highball, those who lowball, and those who are so precise they quote down to the nickel. Some people like to quote the **"suggested retail price"** instead of what they actually paid. When someone **"Asks,"** what kind of information are they looking for anyway?

Julianne's Incident: Bling-Bling

Before Meredith was about to become engaged, she asked to try on my wedding ring. Slipping my ring on her finger, she looked at me directly and said, "It's perfect, what size is it?" When I mumbled 3, she burst into laughter and said, "Not the size of the diamond ding-bat, the size of the ring."

Diamond rings in general are a packed with innuendo and assumption. They seem to symbolize more than just eternal love. (Thanks to Debeer's clever ad campaigns). Engagement rings now infer everything from how serious the relationship is, to how much he loves you, to WHAT DOES HE DO FOR A LIVING? That's right, in this case, the bigger, well, the bigger. Diamonds are a girl's best friend though, right?

> **Rule 16:**
> Talking about money can be hazardous to your health.

"Why do we want to have a lot of money anyway?

It's interesting that people continue to play the lottery even though there are direct correlations to winning and depression, bankruptcy and even suicide.** That's right, suicide. Although you won't hear these stories on the six o'clock news, for fear of people not continuing to play, but there are several cases where the individual, after winning a large sum of money, actually takes their own life. The reports suggest that the never ending focus regarding having so much money becomes overwhelming, stressful and down right exhausting. They loose friendships, marriages and sometimes family relationships do to the riches.

Ways to Make Money:
Earn It! Marry It! Inherit It! Win It!

There was never a time period more notorious for talking about money than during the boom of the early 2000's. Everyone was a **MOP** (millionaire on paper), overnight. And people weren't shy about letting you know how much they were worth from their "initial purchase option" of buying and vesting in stock. But as quickly as it came, it went. Soon the streets were littered with the 𝕭𝕺𝕻's (broke on paper.) The loose talk about net worth was quickly halted. Guess it's no fun to illuminate lean times, unless you're someone who finds enjoyment crying poverty.

Rule 17: Avoid "Crying Poverty" at all cost. It puts you under a microscope of scrutiny. You don't want people questioning every purchase you make because you've cried wolf too many times.

Crying poverty is a pet peeve. It is right up there with people who refer to themselves in the first person, individuals who don't know how to merge onto a freeway, and having someone give commentary during a movie. Sure we all go through tight times, but announcing it and making others feel uncomfortable is truly unnecessary. Especially, when it's not the case and becomes redundant. It cracks us up when someone who cries poverty doesn't have enough money to buy a big gulp, but is driving around in a new Mercedes.

There are times when chattering about money is a simple reaction of not knowing how to say thank you. We find

46

ourselves price dropping when someone compliments us on something. *"Oh, that shirt is really cute."* Instead of just saying thank you, we will typically get a horrible case of diarrhea of the mouth and rattle on about what a bargain it was, *"I know, $16 dollars for a blouse, can you believe it?"* We're not intentionally trying to be a Price Dropper, and clearly judging from the low price of the item we're not bragging about how rich we are, we just find ourselves getting excited over a deal and love to share. However, this altruistic approach can leave people with the wrong impression.

Heidi's Incident: Blue Light Special

A few years back at a New Year's Eve party a few ladies commented on how they loved my fur stole (got it at a flee market for a hundred bucks), loved my shoes (DSW a mere $29), and who does my nails (oh, you must go to True Nails because a manicure and pedicure is only twenty dollars total!) When one of the girls turned away and mumbled, **"Gee,** everything has a price," I realized that my over zealous approach to bargain shopping was leaving people with the wrong idea. **Geeze,** all I wanted to do was simply pass the word.

Are there ever times when it's okay to discuss money? Talk about finances? Have conversation over prices? And, is it ever appropriate, polite or in good taste to be able to discuss money or ask the cost of something?

We say yes . . . gingerly. There are certain

relationships, close friendships or family members where we get to just put etiquette aside and be direct. Know your audience, although the comfort level may be present, so may another unwelcome guest . . . the green-eyed monster. Jealousy has a way of infiltrating even the most banal of conversations.

> **Rule 18:** If you MUST know the cost of something, be careful how you ask. There is a difference between looking for advice, and appearing nosey.

On a final note:

We've heard the expression **"he can afford it"** used

more than once, and felt that it was worth addressing. A friend of ours is often the recipient of people's preconceived notion that he will pick up the tab. One smug guy approached him in the parking lot following a dinner and casually inquired, "Hey Earl, what do I owe you?" "You don't owe *me* anything. But you owe the restaurant about $45 bucks."

Rule 19: it is rude, poor etiquette and bad manners to ever utter the words, "they can afford it."

Tips at a Glance

❖ Don't be Price Dropper

❖ Limit amount of Asking

❖ Careful of the green-
    eyed monster

❖ Never make money
    assumptions

"Buck Up!"
Tipping

<u>Here's a Tip</u>: After self tanning, put rubbing alcohol on a cotton swab and run around your cuticles. This simple trick will help eliminate the appearance of orange dipped fingers.

In Flight Entertainment: Heidi's Layover Nightmare

I'm lying awake in my hotel room. There's so much noise from the band outside I don't think I could hear a fire alarm if it went off in the building. In fact, I don't think I'd hear the alarm if the fire *started* in my room. Tossing, turning, and increasingly uncomfortable swaddled in my stiff paper-thin-25-thread-count-sheets, I glance over and see the 1960's style TV console chained to the moss green carpeted floor that only produces three channels. (Wow, the airlines spare no expense on layover hotels.) Bound and determined to make the best of things, I ingeniously figured out that by doing a little leg stretch I could push the buttons on the TV with my toes. If I could actually get TV reception of the Letterman Show, I'm sure he'd love to see my stupid human toe trick.

With my sleepless night behind me, (at 5 a.m. the band on the beach wrapped it up and I was only left with the drunkin' howls of wild scholars trying to make their last-ditch effort to bag the girl they thought was a 2 at 10 and then a 10 at 2. It's spring break, loneliness is not an option). I made my way through the littered hallway to the lobby where I ordered a large cup of coffee and bran muffin. I gave the waitress, who looked like she had just rolled out of bed herself, wearing a tattered wrinkled uniform with tag stating her name, Vera from Ft. Meyers, the exact total she quoted. No need to do the quick tip tally since in Daytona Beach gratuity is always included (college kids don't get tipping). For a split second I was back in college during spring break, free spirited, wrinkle free and wondering what school the cute guy in the green OP shorts was from. Kicking over a lone can of Pabst Blue Ribbon, I fell back into reality. I handed the waitress another two bucks knowing that not one of these kids would think to add a little extra, and with a mixed look of gratitude and exhaustion, she smiled. I secretly wished they would add a class on tipping into every freshman curriculum. It may not have helped Vera get her groove back but would give insight into a topic which is in desperate need of education.

All the reasons to give a big tip: (think...)

Great service.

Extra long massage.

Next available appointment.

Especially fast currier deliveries.

Requested song actually played by D.J.

On the ball valet who parks your sports -car close.

Unusually straight blow-out that lasts for more than a day.

Sparkly bows put on Fido's ears rather than the plain ones.

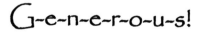

G-e-n-e-r-o-u-s!

Quick Tip: Many times gratuities can be left on credit cards or deducted from Debit cards. It's also a great idea to bring about $40 in small change before a trip, so you're prepared the minute you land at your destination (you'll be ready for the cab driver, bell hop, or doorman.)

Rule 20: compensate service industry workers who you solicit.

With rolling luggage, you can easily handle your own bags, but if you choose to be escorted to your room while the bell boy is schlepping your oversized Samsonite, you should give him a gratuity.

The same goes for hailing a city cab. You can either stand in the rain yourself, or give the doorman a few bucks to flag down a taxi while you stay warm and dry.

How about the pizza delivery person? Similar principle: The pizza is the same price whether or not you have it delivered. The *service* for having it brought, piping hot, to your door is worth giving the driver a few dollars, and much more convenient than picking it up yourself. All you have to do is peel yourself off the couch.

Learning the etiquette of tipping is confusing enough, not to mention the innuendos they imply. Like it or not, gratuity styles will reflect on an individual's character. We have all heard the stories of the generous tippers in <u>Star</u> magazine. Ben Affleck is notorious for playing high stakes poker at casinos but leaving generous tips is where he wins big with the dealers. Also newsworthy (and even juicier) are the stories of the stars who are known to under tip or, God forbid . . . stiff! Ladies, let's not look at tipping as an impossible code to decipher, but a potential perk that could give us a little **bonus!**

Rule 21: Private services should render special attention. The woman scrubbing our feet during a pedicure, a masseuse giving us an intimate full-body massage, or being spread eagle on our esthetician's spa table, enduring a Brazilian Bikini Wax, is not a good time to skimp on a tip, especially if you are having these services done on a regular basis. **Trust us.** When they get "down and dirty" with you, they deserve a little something extra.

Julianne's Incident: Generosity Begets Generosity

This happened not long ago on a romantic get-a-way to New York City with my husband. Staying at a posh hotel on the Upper East Side the bell boy showed us around our tiny, although elegant, standard room, my disappointment was unmistakable. "It's New York; it's the location that really matters," my husband reaffirmed me while handing the bell boy a $20 bill. Having heard this, and realizing his tip had no correlation to our disappointment; the bell boy called his supervisor and managed to upgrade us **(at no additional cost)** to a magnificent suite over looking Central Park!

Lesson learned: it never hurts to be gracious and generous!

The Dreaded Math Word Problem

How much do we tip? Most of us know there is a standard 15%-20% gratuity within the U.S. But what you may not realize is that at the end of each shift, waiters tally every check and must report 12% to Uncle Sam as taxable income (this percentage varies from state to state). For example, Joe the waiter serves a total of $1000 dollars of food and beverages during his shift. He is required to report $120 of assumed tips to the IRS as earned income. Essentially if Joe was stiffed by a customer, he is actually paying taxes on declared income he never received. Plus, in most restaurants, waiters are also required to give a percentage of tips to busboys, hostesses, and bar staff. Although this may sound like a math word problem, the idea is to understand exactly where your tip goes.

> **Rule 22:** Don't get stuck in a tipping rut. People have a tendency to hold fast and furious to their individual tipping habits. We are ladies of the 21st century; we don't want to be in a time warp...right?

A common misconception: However generous our husbands may be, they refuse to tip their hairdresser. Their cut takes 15 minutes and when they do the math, they believe the stylist makes more than a corporate lawyer.

BUT: While this argument may appear to be valid, the calculation doesn't include the amount paid to the salon; such as station rental, product costs, and other overhead expenses.

> **Rule 23:** Keep in mind what the server is actually responsible for. A server being inconsiderate, rude or incompetent is completely different from you not liking how much garlic was in the mashed potatoes. We once saw a sign in a bar that read "If you're drinking to forget, tip me now!" Don't dock their pay for things they aren't responsible for.

Heidi's Incident: The Quarter

No circumstance is more debated than when an expensive bottle of wine is ordered. One February I visited New Orleans during the infamous Mardi Grais celebration. Our group was anxious to sample the local Cajun cuisine in the French Quarter. As we ordered our jambalaya and crawfish ettoufe, one couple recommended we complement our meal with a beautiful bottle of Cabernet Sauvignon. Although this reserve bottle was an expensive indulgence, it enhanced the cayenne spice and was well worth the price. The waiter carefully opened the magnum and poured it into an exquisite decanter. We savored every drop and lingered over the last glass while discussing the colorful traditions of showing **"boobs for beads"** on Bourbon Street.

When the bill arrived, our lively discussion turned into a full-blown debate over how much we should tip. Because the wine was more than half our bill, the question arose: Do you still tip the standard 15%-20% on the entire bill? Several people thought we did not need to leave such a hefty amount given the alcohol was a substantial portion of the bill total. **You may not like this, but you're going to have to tip on that wine. If you can afford the high priced wine, you can afford to tip the waiter accordingly.**

"So what do you do when someone generously pays the entire bill, but shorts the waiter on the gratuity?"

There are two possible answers:

One, is to genuinely thank your host and chalk it up to an honest mistake. You would not want to insult them by calling attention to their faux pas. Maybe they misread the bill and added the numbers incorrectly. Let's give our dining companions the benefit of the doubt. If you feel that this may be a trend, offer to leave the tip yourself. (Food for thought, this could offend the person offering to pay, be prepared.)

Two, is to *covertly* enhance the tip. (DO NOT GET CAUGHT!) When Julianne's grandmother was alive, she used to take her to her favorite café for lunch. Grandma would order the same cup of clam chowder with a half an egg salad sandwich every Friday. No matter what the bill came to, at 87 years old she felt leaving two shiny quarters was an ample tip. We love Grandma, but her old school standard of tipping was leaving the young waiter less than satisfied.

Julianne tried insisting on paying the bill or at least leaving the tip, but Grandma wouldn't hear of it. She finally realized her only option was to get sneaky. After she helped Grandma into the car, got her buckled and stored her walker in the trunk, she would always seem to forget her sunglasses on the table. Julianne would run back into the restaurant to retrieve her specs and slip the waiter a little extra tip along with a knowing wink.

"What should I do when I'm traveling abroad?"

Familiarize yourself with local standards. For example, certain countries have a "no tip" standard; however, they know Americans *do* tip and look forward to it. Other countries may view a gratuity as an insult, so you're better off not tipping. It never hurts to ask. If you are uncomfortable asking your server, inquire with the hostess, receptionist, or concierge on acceptable tipping procedures.

"When in Doubt . . . Ask."

Rule 24: Know who to tip. As times change, so does the tipping industry. People such as contractors, gardeners, and dance club DJ's are among the lengthy list of possible recipients. **WOW!**

We realize that the list gets pretty lengthy when you start adding in all possible gratuity recipients. Going to the Coffee House every day is a prime example of how awkward it gets at the register when the plastic tip jar is staring you in the face as if to say **"feed me!"** It's hard to pay for an overpriced cup of java and then have to tip in addition. But then you look at these hard working kids, trying to earn a couple of bucks the old fashion way and you realize, "what's the big deal to toss in the change for the starving college student who is doing their best to make me that perfect mocha?"

The bottom line: The left over change will have more of a positive impact for them than for you.

Unfortunately not all employees' receive a salary. For some, a gratuity becomes their primary source of income. Heidi's brother worked as a valet parking cars and never received a paycheck: he was solely working for tips. Running back and forth in the hot Arizona sun was made even more miserable when monetary acknowledgements were not given. Kevin would laugh at the irony of the businessman driving the S class Mercedes, appearing preoccupied to avoid looking him in the eye, and handing him a buck, while the guy driving the pale yellow K car would give him a five spot **(and a smile)**. What once may have been a complimentary service may now be an industry which is compensated solely by gratuities.

Indeed tipping is a complicated practice and many people have strong opinions about this topic. For example, I have listened to several arguments between individuals discussing whether or not to tip on the *total* or *subtotal* of a bill. Usually an extra dollar or two means the difference between walking away looking cheap, or leaving looking like a hero. If you've had a pleasant experience, put the tip chart down (actually burn it) and **error on the side of generosity.**

Rule 25: Round up, just a bit, and both you and your server will have a better experience.

Tips at a Glance

❖ Tipping generously benefits everyone

❖ Tip individuals whose service we request

❖ In general, 15%-20% is standard for most service industries

❖ When in doubt, ask

❖ Error on the side of generosity

"Here comes the Bill!"
Weddings

In Flight Entertainment: Turbulence

Allison was a fellow flight attendant who married a First Officer only a few months prior. Yes, it's as predictable as the cheerleader-football player arrangement, and yes, they made an equally picture perfect couple. This was why it was odd that we didn't recognize her at first in her baggy uniform and sullen-pale skin. We assumed she must have just come from the Frankfurt all-nighter. Octoberfest layovers (among other circumstances) have a way of making flight attendants look like they've aged ten years overnight. "Guten morgen, how is the new Mrs. Johnson," Heidi gingerly asked, still concerned over her new heroin-chic look. It was apparent that she'd asked the wrong question when Allison's eyes welled up, she bowed her head and whispered, "I guess the urban legend is true, although he didn't have a girl in every port, just one in Cleveland of all places...it's over." Wow, didn't see that one coming. "Oh my gosh, I can't believe it," Heidi consoled. (In retrospect he *was* notorious for indoctrinating new stews into the mile high club.) "I'm so sorry, what a jerk, I hate him...**Hey, listen, do you think I could get my gift back?"**

There was a time in our lives when nothing evoked such grand feelings of hope, love and future than weddings. We were thrilled to receive wedding invitations from our friends. The smell of freshly cut flowers, the gentle sounds of a four-string quartette and the rich fabrics (embossed with crystals and pearls) always excited us. Weddings represented all that was good in life; **good food, good wine and good people**. They were the reflection of every young girl's dream of becoming a bride in a magnificent gown and cathedral length veil, walking down the aisle toward Prince Charming's waiting arms.

Rule 26: Don't Forget the Guest. There are plenty of wedding books and magazines that assist in planning the perfect wedding. This chapter is a departure from traditional wedding etiquette books because it focuses on an aspect of expense that most engaged couples overlook **the guest.**

Do you ever think weddings in general have lost the essence of why we have a ceremony? That the average couple spends approximately eighteen months planning their wedding, but less than an hour planning their marriage, illuminates the fact that marketers are doing their job in making us believe this notion, "The grander the celebration, the more important the marriage." Celebrities who've spent millions on their nuptials, just to divorce several months later, are a prime example of how the cost of a wedding and the longevity of marriage do not necessarily correlate. Yes, it stinks when a couple doesn't make it to their one year anniversary after going through the detailed process of having a wedding, but it especially stings the guest who bucked up several hundred dollars (if not thousands) to support the cause. This may not be a popular opinion, but engaged couples should take a step back from the wedding frenzy and approach their day as if they were hosting someone at their home. Ideally, guests should remember how amazing you looked in your dress, how delicious the food was and what a spectacular evening they had, not the fact that they had to hawk their grandmother's broach to finance their attendance.

"But isn't this MY day?"

Overindulging on your special day is fine, if you (or your parents) have the means to cover the expense. But, be careful of etiquette faux pas lurking around every corner and tempting the unsuspecting bride.

"Until Debt Do We Part."

The Cost of Being a Guest

At the minimum, everyone must bring a wedding gift. Additional expenditures may include (hold your breath): Attire (tux rental, bridesmaid gown or appropriate wedding outfit including shoes and accessories), engagement parties (another gift), showers (gift, decorations and possible money if you host the event), bachelor/bachelorette party (another possible gift, night out of entertainment, possible weekend away), money for the reception (no host bar, money dance, or parking), hotel (especially if the wedding is out-of-town), and miscellaneous items (limos, airfare, or rental car). Yikes!

RULE 27: To the future Mr. and Mrs.: make sure that when budgeting for your wedding you're not financially impacting your *guests.*

Somebody needs to remind the bride and groom that there's a reason we call it a "guest" and not "hey-do-you-mind-pitching-in-and-paying-for-part-of-my-vision" person.

There are several examples of how guests are impacted. The most obvious and popular scheme is to eliminate the **"open bar."** It seems that nixing the "open bar" has become an acceptable expenditure that is cut. We are not suggesting that you must pay for your guests to have alcohol, and it's perfectly fine not to serve booze at your reception, but if you want your guests to have the option of indulging in spirits, then the reality is you should foot the bill. We like to use the analogy: If you invite people over to your house for dinner, would you make them pay for their own drinks? We are just waiting for the day when we're sitting at a reception and the

69

server offers us chicken or steak, but if we choose the cow it will cost us $15.00!

> **Rule 28**: You shouldn't offer something then expect your guests to have to pay.

"Have your cake and eat it, too!"

> **RULE 29**: Don't choose something which saves you money, but ultimately becomes an expense for your guests. Choosing to have a Friday wedding in order to rent the reception hall for half price is a frugal alternative. Please realize that expecting your guests to take time off work in order to make the festivities is actually impacting *them*.

Julianne's Incident: Bridal Showers

I must confess I made this mistake at my own wedding. Because my fiancé and I were paying for the shindig ourselves, we were concerned about not getting carried away with spending too much on a day that lasts only a few hours. Truth be told, we decided a ten-day extravagant honeymoon in Tahiti would be a better use of our money. Unfortunately, it turns out payback really was and is a biAtch. We landed in Bora Bora smack in the middle of a monsoon that lasted our entire trip. Every day we would go to the front desk to ask the receptionist for the forecast on the primitive island, and every day she would arch her neck around the counter, peek outside and say, "It look-a-like-a-rain." Maybe if we had used our money hosting our guests properly instead of splurging on a tropical honeymoon for ourselves, Karma wouldn't have reared its ugly head. It wasn't our intention to be poor "hosts," honestly I never realized I was supposed to be the host...wasn't it all about me, my day?

The average person will spend approximately $20,000 on their wedding. Flip through any bride's magazine and you will be bombarded with propaganda marketing all of the wedding must haves. Designer gowns, large diamond rings, and exotic honeymoons are just a few essentials that can suck a bank account dry. Slogans that promote "a-once-in-a-lifetime day," propel us into spending more than many people make in an entire year. A friend of ours chose to forgo buying a house in order to afford the $100,000 fantasy wedding she had dreamed of for years. Understandably, it's hard not to want to splurge when you are making the biggest commitment of your life.

RULE 30: If you have your heart set on the gals wearing a designer gown with a higher than average price tag, help pay for it. One groom creatively exchanged his credit card mileage and sprung for his usher's designer tuxedos.

"Always a Bridesmaid..."

The Big White Lie:
"After the wedding, you can cut off the bridesmaid dress and make it into a cocktail dress"

Julianne was at a wedding once and saw a girl sitting in the pew wearing a fuchsia colored knee-length dress. "That's an old bridesmaid gown," She whispered to her husband. Seconds later when the processional began a stream of hot pink made its way down the aisle (yes, same dress only it hadn't yet been converted). Luckily it was a Catholic mass so the girl looked like she was prolonging her genuflect instead of trying to be incognito. Mortified, the girl showed up to the reception in a different ensemble.

We've never understood why girls wear the exact dress anyhow; don't they try to avoid this at all costs in Hollywood? What dress style looks good on everyone? And if you're not the one who looks best in the dress, regardless of your age, it stinks. One of the most beautiful wedding parties we've ever seen was bridesmaids all in satin (different styles and pastel colors), and groomsmen in their own dark suits. What tied the attendants together were the matching bouquets of flowers for the girls and pale satin neckties for the men. **It was an outstanding display of individuality while keeping with the continuity of the wedding party.**

> **Rule 31:** When picking attire for wedding attendants, be respectful of how far you're expecting them to dig into their wallet. Even the most beautiful bridesmaid dress will never be worn again. Repeat after us: "It Will NEVER be worn again."

Heidi's Incident: Shopaholic

I couldn't wait to register for gifts. There was nothing quite like walking around a store with a price gun, swiping skew numbers and creating a wish list for my new married life. Unsure of which china, crystal and stemware patterns to select, the bubbly salesgirl directed me to the stores highest-end items advising, "Don't worry about prices, people will buy whatever piece of the place setting they can afford." Ohhh, music to my ears, I liked this girl. I quickly picked out my dream Waterford wine glasses, thinking nothing of the ridiculous price tag. If that wasn't enough, I also took the salesgirl's advice to register for outrageous items. She mused at how generous people are when it comes to weddings stating, "You never know what people will buy." I selected a Dior luggage set, a Faberge Egg and a Mink duvet cover, never realizing that I could be leaving my guests with the impression that I was greedy. By the way, in case you're tempted, no one sprung for the Egg or the Mink. But I am now the proud owner of a Dior train case.

74

RULE 32: Don't ask for someone to buy you a home. A new trend for the wedding registry is to open an account at a mortgage company in the engaged couple's name. Guests are asked to make donations toward a down payment for the newlywed's house in lieu of a wedding gift. Bottom line: it's just tacky.

If you thought the "white wedding" was the only style of reception that could trigger poor money manners, think again. The **"destination wedding"** has become a popular alternative for the cosmopolitan couple. The idea of exchanging vows on the cliffs of San Tropez sounds delightful. This alternative to the church wedding can be a win-win situation; the bride and groom can combine the expense of a wedding with the honeymoon, and the guests get to have a fantastic vacation. However, although destination weddings are gaining notoriety, they may also become a HUGE expense to guests.

"Barefoot In a Bikini!"

Rule 33: Change your expectation of attendance if you choose a destination wedding. Don't take it personally if people can't afford the trip. Plus, if you're not having to worry about all the extra people, you can focus you're attention to you and your beloved. How fabulous!

When it comes to destination weddings, traditional invitations make people feel obligated to attend. Our favorite destination wedding invitation we ever received was from a girlfriend who announced to friends and family that she was planning on getting married in Maui. She did not send formal invitations, but instead revealed her decision verbally. "Anyone who wants to attend is more than welcome." For those looking for a good excuse to go to Hawaii, it was fantastic; however, it didn't obligate others who couldn't afford the expensive trip.

RULE 34: Spring for certain amenities to soften the financial blow for your guests.

We attended one wedding where the bride and groom meticulously made sure that their guest *felt* like a guest. Shuttles were provided to and from the airport and reception sites, which was also the perfect excuse for everyone to get loose at the reception. Breakfast certificates to the hotel restaurant and amenity baskets were placed in each room. A welcome bonus when we woke up feeling a bit hazy was finding a much-needed bottle of Tylenol by the bed. An additional touch was **including out-of-town guests at their rehearsal dinner** (some have overlooked this courtesy). It wasn't surprising that the first dance for the newlyweds was "Be our Guest" from Beauty and the Beast. They really nailed it.

Tips at a Glance

❖ Don't make a budget that benefits you but costs your guests

❖ Register for moderately priced items

❖ Be respectful of the out-of-town guests' expenses

❖ Remember you're the host

"The Boondoggle"
Stealing from friends and family

In Flight Entertainment: Bon Voyage!

There is an urban legend about two flight attendants who skimmed so much cash from collecting liquor and amenity money on the airplane that they had enough to buy a yacht which they appropriately named "Head Set." This cleared up any question we used to have as to why all the senior flight attendants wanted to work coach. Apparently the airline never made the connection to the multitude of "comped" drinks and the low revenue collected on flights. Executives must have thought there were a lot of disgruntled passengers. Meanwhile, two very sneaky stews were enjoying the azure seas.

"What's a Boondoggle?"

A boondoggle is when you pass off personal perks as a business expense. (Like an exotic trip to Asia to see a "client.") It could also be expensing a dinner to your company when the reality is it was you and you best friend enjoying a feast. Or maybe you used the company suite tickets for your hot date last Friday. Simply put, it's capitalizing off of others. EEW!

"How did we learn to capitalize off others?

Julianne's Incident: The Birth of a Boondoggle

I recall being sixteen and my parents providing me with a Chevron Card. My friends and I would all pile into my parent's station wagon (complete with wood-sided paneling).

We would cruise around town, hitting all the Taco Bell's and trying to find the senior parties. At some point, a collection would take place to chip in for the gas. Even though gas was only about a buck a gallon, often the pot would be as much as five or six dollars. That's a lot of petrol. More to the point, I wasn't even paying for the fuel . . . I had the Chevron Card, remember? I would keep the dough and treat myself to the new "Wham!" cassette. Was that so wrong?

Our parents are often the initial victim of the boondoggle. In college there were several stories of people taking the gas card scam to a whole new level. Students would register for an extra class, have their parents pay the tuition, later drop the course and pocket the refund. One guy found a drinking hole that had an ambiguous name called "The College Stop." He would rack up enormous bar bills, often offering to buy drinks for an entire sorority (this, of course, enhanced his popularity making him the BIGGEST man on campus). It wasn't until graduation that his father figured out that "The College Stop" wasn't a bookstore and that he had been footing his son's bar bill for *four* years.

Rule 35: Don't boondoggle your parents. Think of all the sleepless nights, endless support, and unconditional love they gave you. If you're reading this, you're all grown up and probably not boondoggling your parents anymore, but if you have children...consider this "friends helping friends" advice. (Not that our little Darlings would ever dream of taking advantage.)

At some point these seemingly harmless **"entitlements"** we take from our parents can evolve into full-blown stealing. Initially the thought of a boondoggle may not seem so bad when it's perceived to be just mom and dad (and you were just a kid), or a faceless entity (like confiscating a few new bath towels from the luxury hotel where you're staying), but when you apply the same principle to a friend or co-worker, it turns personal. This unbelievably happens more than you might think.

Heidi's Incident: The Butt of the Boondoggle

As a flight attendant, we often shared an entire month of dining with our crewmembers. One particular month in Boise, the crew found a perfect little joint with good Italian food and great atmosphere. Towards the end of each meal, we would tally up our portion and the pilot would collect our cash and put the entire amount on his credit card--a frequent practice in dining.

It wasn't until the end of the month, when our service had progressively declined, that one flight attendant confronted the owner as to why this was the case. She was flabbergasted to find out that the server had only been tipped 5% throughout the month. This baffled her because after each meal she remembered crewmembers including at least 20% gratuity on their tally. The pilot had pulled the most hideous of boondoggles, capitalizing off his fellow co-workers. He had pocketed the cash which had included our 20% tip. I understand corporate cut-backs and tight times, but this was **despicable!**

There is nothing more corrupt than to combine pilfering from your company **and** stealing from friends. We call this double dipping (not the kind where you dip your chip into the guacamole twice), but the kind where you benefit simultaneously from both parties (like collecting money from your dining companions for a meal you're intending to expense.)

Rule 36: Double Dipping is Hideous.
There is never an excuse to capitalize off your friends.

Confessions of a Double Dipper

I didn't start out with the intention to capitalize off my friends, it just sorta happened. I was right out of college and landed my dream sales job with a huge expense account. I was encouraged to wine and dine clients and spare no expense. It didn't take long for me to realize that the accounting department (understaffed and overworked) didn't keep close tabs on what, who and where my expenses were going. At first it was just a lunch with a girlfriend here, or a drink with a boyfriend there. It became almost second nature for me to whip out my company card and pick up the tab. One night several of my closest gals got together for dinner to celebrate one of our birthdays. The bill was ENORMOUS, we didn't skimp on anything. As usual, I gave the waitress my company card and expensed the ENTIRE bill. A few moments later, people started handing me cash, and a lot of it. I tried to say "no, don't worry about it" but they wouldn't hear of me picking up the tab. I got embarrassed to tell them that I was charging it to my company. What would they think of me? I kept quiet and pocketed the cash. What's worse is after that night, my double-dipping became more frequent. It was easy to put an entire bill on my card then pocket my chum's cash. I justified this by saying, "They'd still be paying the same amount regardless of who takes their cash." It wasn't until I got fired for "misuse of expense account" that I realized... THERE ARE NO SELF HELP PROGRAMS FOR DOUBLE DIPPERS!

Sincerely,

Anonymous

Temptation often prevails over the social graces of money. Whether it's lobbying for company season box tickets and then selling them on the side to your neighbors, or lying to the waiter about it being your birthday just to satisfy your after lunch sweet-tooth, IT'S STILL A BOONDOGGLE!

"DON'T LET THE Fancy TERM FOOL YOU!"

Although boondoggling may seem funny, playful or even crafty, at the end of the day it is really no different than slipping your neighbors knick-knack in your pants and walking out the door. Outrageous? Yes. But when you think about it, the principle is the same.

> **Rule 37:** Capitalizing off
>
> of someone else's generosity
>
> is not gracious or ethical.

The Unintentional Boondoggle: Opps, He Did it Again!

Every now and again a boondoggle occurs without an initial intent to do so. We are certain this was the case when the check came at a friend's birthday dinner. Awkward because we didn't know if her husband was picking up the tab given there were written invitations involved. Not wanting to be presumptuous, a few of us asked how much we owed. The problem was the ambiguity of Mack's response, "Oh, whatever you want." Still feeling unsure, one couple handed him a $100. Looking at the bill he shook his head, **"Wow, that's too much."** But proceeded to combined it with the cash in his hand and didn't offer any change. Other couples started handing him stacks of cash. Same exchange. He would say "No, no, that's too much," but then nonchalantly include it to the take. The entire focus becomes the bill and watching him count this enormous stack of cash. In the end, Mack pays the check and pockets the rest of the change. Yes, he did. But no, he didn't intend to Boondoggle.

Tips at a Glance

❖ Use judgment when using company perks

❖ "Double Dipping" is hideous

❖ Don't jeopardize ethics for a freebie

❖ Never capitalize off of friends

"Sugar Daddy!"
Giving Gifts

In Flight Entertainment: It's a Zoo!

We're trained professionals: with one eye we can
continue to make a pre-departure gin and tonic and with the
other, we can sum up the exact overhead bin space still
available. It's the crew's sixth sense. So when we saw the
enormous giraffe **piñata** making his way down the jet bridge,
it was clear there was going to be a discrepancy. "Ma'me,
we're going to have to check your, uh, carry-on." The
passenger, who apparently had purchased the monstrosity at
a local market, would not waiver. It was a gift for her young
son's birthday and if put below it would surely break. The
gate agent standing behind the woman (and giraffe) had a "I

told you they wouldn't let that thing on the plane" look on her face. Boarding was at a standstill. We didn't want to rob a little boy of his birthday surprise, but there just wasn't a closet big enough to hold the thing. "You can strap him in a seat" the premium first-class flight attendant offered jokingly. The agent, obviously done with this whole issue, ran with the idea, "Yes, we have a **FIRST** class seat available." Needless to say Mr. Giraffe, occupying 4B, had a fantastic flight which included a pillow and blanket, hot nuts, and a cold gin and tonic!

Gifts can be a sensitive subject. You do all this work, painstakingly picking out just the right thing and it never fails, after the short moment of **oohing** and **aahing**, it gets tossed into a pile and immediately dismissed as the next gift takes precedent. **It can hurt a girl's feelings.**

Rule 38: It is, and always will be, the thought that counts. It may be cliché, but it's true.

Heidi's story: Frostbite

My last attempt at participating in Christmas went a little
something like this: 6:30 a.m. It's Christmas morning. I felt
like a kid again, running down the stairs to start the fire, turn
the CD player to some soft holiday carols, pour OJ into my
barely used crystal glasses. 7:30: I open the door to the kids'
rooms and turn on some hall lights. No movement. I turn on
more lights and blow my already dry hair. Still nothing. 8:00:
I turn up the music and change the CD to Harry Connick Jr.'s
Christmas Blues. Nothing. 8:15: Now desperate, I shake my
husband out of his deep slumber "Let me sleep a little longer"
he mumbles groggily. **"You've got to be kidding, it's
Christmas morning, doesn't anyone in this house want to
celebrate this damn holiday?"**
8:30: Change the CD and crank up Fifty Cent Gangsta' Rap
Christmas. Still plugging away, I force everyone up and I coax
them to the living room. My husband and children open
their mound of presents. My plastic smile beginning to fade
just as my youngest asks, "What did Santa bring mom?" My
husband looks at me baffled, "What? You said you didn't
want anything."

The pressure of gift giving can make you feel more
confined than being midway through an MRI and having an
itch. How much to spend, when should we give, and when is

enough-enough, are constant points of despair that can boggle even the most contemporary of minds. Gift registries make coming up with "what" to buy easy, but we often wonder what the underlying message is when giving gifts from a registry. "Congratulations on your nuptials, here's a fork." Now every time they sit down and indulge in a piece of key lime pie, do they think of you?

"What Do you want for your Birthday?"

Julianne's Incident: Pyramid Scheme

The last time I felt the pressure of how complicated gift giving can be was when my girlfriend showed up to my baby shower with a stack (in pyramid formation) of presents. Astounded at the monstrosity, I was even more shocked when she set the gifts down, went back out to her car and pulled in an additional wagon full (seriously, a red wagon overloaded with toys.) I made a mental note to self: return Baby Einstein video I was planning to give her the following week for her shower (here I thought I was so original not giving the Diaper

Genie), go to bank, transfer funds to pay for new gift, and cancel lunch on Tuesday (seems I was going to spend my afternoon at Baby's r Us).

Common Questions:

How much should I spend? The amount you want to spend on a gift really depends on your personal budget. JLo can afford to buy Bentleys for her boyfriends, but most of us live on a fairly tight budget that rarely includes expensive gifts. We tend to spend more on close relationships than we spend on acquaintances. On average, most people will spend between $25 and $50 on a gift for an individual, and double the amount for a couple.

When should I buy a gift? You should give a gift if you are invited to a party, luncheon, or dinner that marks an occasion. If you are not planning on seeing the person around the special date, then send a card or leave a thoughtful message. What is the point of bringing a November birthday gift to someone on Valentine's Day? The moment has passed. Our busy schedules don't always allow us to celebrate *every* occasion with *every* person.

Who should I buy a gift for? As we get older and our family and circle of friends grow, giving gifts to everyone and their children becomes a daunting and expensive task. It's not necessary to buy gifts for every occasion & for every person we know. There are plenty of creative and inexpensive ways to acknowledge an event that does not include purchasing a gift. We LOVE a simple phone call on our birthday from loved ones.

Rule 39: Spend what you can afford and feel good about. You should never feel pressured to purchase more than your budget. Let's always remember: The best gifts come from the heart.

Great Idea:
The Token Gift!

Tokens are just a little something that lets them know you're thinking about them and want to acknowledge the event. Items such as a fun faux pair of earrings, a holiday ornament, this book for example, or a fresh bouquet of flowers are all appropriate and thoughtful ways of sending the message that you care. It doesn't have to be expensive. A night of babysitting, a home cooked meal, or sharing a talent are all possibilities. One of our favorite gifts is still breakfast in bed. (Our husbands will read this and be so excited ... no, you are not off the hook because we still like jewelry, too!)

When you're a child, there is nothing quite like the excitement of a present. As an adult, "buy me a drink," and skip the basket of scented vanilla lotion. The important thing is celebrating occasions together, not feeling the pressure of the whole "gift" hoo ha. This is probably why parents always stress to their children, "Don't buy me a gift, just do well in school."

The Bait and Switch

We received a beautifully engraved invitation to a girlfriend's birthday party with a note on the bottom stating "no gifts, please." Following the host's specific directions we came strolling through the entry hall carrying only a witty card (something about a trouser press and wrinkles, super funny). Our confidence turned to embarrassment when we tripped over the gift table stacked with mounds of beautifully wrapped presents. In a panic, Julianne defended herself, "I swear the invite said no gifts." We stuck our card on the bottom secretly hoping nobody would notice.

Rule 40: Print "No gifts, please" at the bottom of the announcement if you are *not* intending for people to send gifts. This is not a trick, so please don't bring one.

Another point we want to address is multi-celebrated events and gift obligations. Two years ago we were invited to a bachelorette party in Cabo San Lucas. It sounded like fun and most of us wanted a good excuse for a girls' weekend away. Our own travel expenses consisted of hotel, air, food, transportation, and entertainment. We were also expected to bring a gift for the bachelorette, chip in for her facial, and share in the cost of a night out (dinner, drinks and a show . . . O.K. it was a strip club, but still). At one point it was tossed around to cover the bride's hotel and airfare. Unfortunately, what we remember from this trip was not the margaritas by the pool, but the pressure to spend more than we felt was reasonable.

"So where *do* you draw the line?"

Rule 41: The responsibility to end the cycle of pressure must fall on the *receiver.* If you're the guest of honor, speak up by saying something like, "Hey, a bachelorette party in Vegas sounds like fun, but expensive. Let me pay my own way."

> # Gifts are just an added bonus...not the focal point!

Have you ever been tempted to re-gift?

What do you do with a gift that doesn't fit, you don't like, or already have? If you don't have the receipt, you can still attempt to return it (if you know where it was purchased), but it doesn't always work. So what do you do if returning the present isn't an option? *Dum-da-dum-dum!*

Some people would never dream of re-gifting, so the gift will sit on a shelf unused until it eventually makes its way to garage sale heaven. But for many of us, it seems a shame to let a perfectly good gift go to waste.

> **Rule 42:** Use a re-gift as a practical solution rather than an intended scam. No one wants to feel duped.

"Is it ever okay to re-gift?"

Ways to Re-gift

The "two-fer", two gifts for the price of one:
Enhance your primary purchase of a sweater by throwing in a re-gifted pair of turquoise earrings you have never worn.

The "windfall", the unnecessary gift: Give the re-gift when you see the infant for the first time. "I had this outfit and thought it would be adorable on little Kyle." (but, don't use the re-gift as a baby shower gift.)

The "hostess trinket", don't show up empty handed: Including a small re- gift with your hors d'oeuvres is always well received. "I thought this frame would look great in your house. Thanks for having me to dinner."

The "gift gratis", a gift to someone you wouldn't normally give to: Someone you don't know well will truly be touched by the thought. Your postal worker, a neighbor you don't normally socialize with, the girl who makes your latte everyday at Starbucks, would be moved at the gesture (regardless if a re-gift is suspected.)

A dear friend of ours is notorious for his generosity. His motto "The joy is in the giving," captures the true spirit of kindness. The process of shopping, selecting, and purchasing a gift should evoke just that . . . **joy.** Make sure you feel good about the presents you give. Give from the heart, and remember, money can buy presents but **not:**

LOVE
FRIENDSHIP
KINDNESS or
PEACE of
MIND!

Tips at a glance

❖ Spend what you feel good about

❖ There are many ways to give

❖ Know when to re-gift

❖ When you are the receiver, alleviate pressure of the giver

"Dig Deep!"
Borrowing Money

In Flight Entertainment: Hot Couture!

The crew was waiting downstairs in the lobby for us. We were changing as fast as we could in order to maximize every minute of our Rio layover. Lucky for Heidi the trip fell on her birthday (nothing like celebrating 29 in Brazil!) As we were doing some last minute primping, Heidi noticed the reflection of another flight attendant holding her brand new dress.

"Can I wear this Heidi-- I hate everything I packed?" This question was unusual for two reasons; One, it was a layover so it wasn't like Heidi had several options. Two, we are certain she was aware of the "golden rule" of clothes swapping...asking to borrow something "new" is off limits. "Uh, well, um I didn't pack another outfit, sorry." The flight attendant glared at Heidi for a brief moment, threw the dress on the bed and shouted, "Fine, FINE! YOU BE THE STAR! How did Heidi become the bad guy for wanting to wear her own dress? Interesting twist. Why do we borrow? It's just problematic.

Let's face it, we live in a world that allows us, almost encourages us, to live beyond our means. We've been living beyond our means since we were young and got our first credit card. We quickly learned the "buy now, pay later" mantra of modern living. We were crafty, too. It didn't take long to figure out the department store credit card also worked as a bank in a pinch. You could buy a gift certificate for $100, purchase the cheapest pair of socks, pocket the change, and be on your way. . "Creative finance!"

For most of us, there are countless times when we are a little short on funds. Have you ever lived by the saying "Robbing Peter to pay Paul?" Sometimes our social life seems to surpass our income level. It's hard saying "no" to a fabulous Sushi dinner or a spontaneous weekend in Mexico. But what happens when the credit cards max out something unforeseen happens?

Julianne's Incident: Stranded

It was all going along swimmingly until my car broke down.
My credit cards were maxed out; I was overextended to
finance a new car, and I obviously didn't have any money in
savings to fix it. I was stranded . . . literally. There was no
alternative but to ask my dad for help. My father is a self-
made man who rose from the obscurity of farming all the way
to middle-class America. He didn't believe in credit cards. "If
you can't afford to pay cash, then you can't afford it," he
would say. Dad always tried to teach us to "paddle our own
canoes" which meant you shouldn't get yourself into a
position where you are *ever* financially dependent on
someone. Oops.

I had no choice but to make the call. "I'll have to think about
it," was his response. The long silence that followed left me
feeling like I had let my Dad down. And trust me, this was
even more painful than having to endure spending my
Saturday visiting every auto parts store price comparing. My
father is the type that will spend five dollars in gas to save
thirty cents on a jar of mayonnaise. That incident made me
realize the residual effect of **help,** may last longer than the
loan itself. To this day, if I show up with anything new, my
father will give me the "are you sure you can afford it" look.

Rule 43: Borrowing from loved ones puts individual relationships at risk. Even if you repay the loan in a reasonable amount of time, the fear of *your* financial instability becomes *their* concern. Once you have borrowed money, your relationship will forever be marked by that event.

If you have ever borrowed money, you can relate to the gut-wrenching feeling of even having to ask. It is humiliating. Still, circumstances arise beyond our control, leaving us with no alternative but to swallow our pride and hunt for funds. The easiest solution is often requesting dough from family (parents, in particular) or friends. While this seems like the path of least resistance, BEWARE!

Rule 44: Don't Ask. No one likes to be asked for a loan. Trust us, it puts people in an awkward position when they are asked by someone they love for money. Remember this if you find yourself tempted to ask your buddy for a boost. We don't want to jeopardize are relationships...right?

A Sad Story

Many personal relationships have been severed because of causal floating of greenbacks. There are several variations of the classic story about the friend "Mooching Marge," who borrowed money from her confidant "Lending Linda." Several months went by with no attempt to repay the loan. Every time the gals would connect, Mooching Marge would show up in a new outfit. Infuriated, Lending Linda could no longer associate with Marge and refused to return her calls. The friendship ended. Ironically, Mooching Marge never remembered borrowing the bundle, and to this day doesn't know why the friendship fizzled.

The moral of this story: If you do find yourself borrowing money, make sure you don't indulge in ANYTHING that could be construed as frivolous until you pay back the loan. Rule 45

This is often tough to do. But, in order to avoid being rude, the person requesting funds must buckle down and make every effort to re-pay the loan . . . **ASAP!** This is especially difficult for large money amounts (like a down payment for a house). There is the notion, when the amount owed is so large that skipping a Saturday matinee will not impact the debt. True that $9 does not make a dent in a $20,000 loan; however, the message you send by pampering yourself may put a dent in your relationship. Does this mean you shouldn't see a movie for the next ten years while you pay back your parents? No, but if you want to avoid being resented at the next Thanksgiving dinner, attempt to pay a little extra each month as a sign of **"good faith."** If you're hunting for money because you've gotten yourself into a pickle, weigh your options carefully. Before you tap your friends and family for a boost, make sure you have exhausted all other possible solutions. Keep in mind, giving you a "free loan" is in essence costing *them* money they could be earning in interest. (Not so "free.")

Do you realize that Egg Donation pays thousands of dollars?

Okay, maybe that's a tad excessive!

Alternative ideas to borrowing:

Increase your credit card limit. It's a simple phone call. Relying on your own resources is always a better alternative than leaning on friendships.

Apply for a personal loan from your bank. This will require you to fill out an application, but banks offer solutions you may not have considered such as a home equity loan, or upping your overdraft protection. It may also be possible to get an advance on your paycheck. If you're really desperate and need something short term, check-cashing services are another alternative.

Sell something. We know people who have generated as much as $800 in a weekend by selling stuff they had around the house! There are also sophisticated alternatives on-line (EBay, Craig's List) that accomplish the same objective.

Earn the money yourself. If your pockets are empty, try raising the funds. You might be amazed to realize hidden talents you have that could yield big profits. A hot commodity for most of the couples we know is overnight or weekend babysitting. Easy Money!

Sometimes borrowing money isn't necessarily a formal transaction. There is a more covert way to "borrow" called mooching. Mooching isn't a sign of ignorance, or forgetfulness. It's a specific personality trait that has no guilt about "taking." We all know people like this. They are notorious for showing up places a little light on cash. You arrive at the local pub, and they say, "Grab us some drinks, I forgot my wallet." We call these people the "nickel and dimers" (although it is always more than just some spare change.) These individuals are not the people who come asking for large scale loans, but the ones who always seem to be a "little short," and we don't mean in height! Picture yourself at the ticket booth of a movie theater. Your friend turns to you as he counts out a few bills and says "Hey, I thought I had more cash on me. Do you have five bucks I can borrow? I'll pay you back tomorrow." The problem is, tomorrow never comes; and it is difficult to ask for the money back.

> **Rule 46:** Mooching is essentially borrowing, so if your pal spots you, make sure to remember to pay them back. **A lender should never have to ask.**

Heidi's Incident: Sneaky Secretary

My husband's secretary asked if we would let her throw her brother's birthday party at our house (hers was under construction.) Of course we said "yes" and made every effort to ensure a memorable evening. Although Judy helped with some details, she never offered to pay for the food, drinks or cake (I found it odd, given the occasion was in honor of her relative.) What really shocked me was when the party was over, she packed up all the left-overs. Initially, I thought she was helping me clean up, but when she transported them to her trunk, I realized she was securing her meals for the next five nights!

One final note about lending money is: ***Don't ever lend an amount that you can't afford to lose.*** Once the cash leaves your hands, there is always the possibility that it may never make its way home. We once heard of a couple who lent their children's entire college fund to a dear friend in need. Apparently the "**dear friend**" had a bit of a gambling problem and lost all of the money before proceeding to declare bankruptcy. The unfortunate couple never did get repaid, and they are still making payments on their children's college loans.

Rule 47: Never lend an amount you can't afford to loose.

Tips at a Glance

❖ Avoid borrowing from friends and family

❖ Borrowing $ will affect personal relationships

❖ Don't be a Mooch

❖ If you do borrow, pay back ASAP

"The Girls" Julianne Pekarthy and Heidi Farr continue their passion for providing money etiquette advice through their free website

www.professormoneymanners.com

They have been guests on several radio and television programs discussing situations where money intersects with personal relationships. Both authors currently reside in Northern California.